BE ANGRY... AND
TRAIN YOUR KIDS

Directing your God-given energy to wisely
fuel godly parenting strategies

By Peggy Ployhar

Peggy Ployhar

Be Angry...And Train Your Kids
Copyright © 2019 by Peggy Ployhar & SPED Homeschool

Edited by Mary Winfield and Tracy Glockle

For information contact :
SPED Homeschool
PO Box 996, Kemah TX 77565
http://spedhomeschool.com/

Book and Cover design by Peggy Ployhar

First Edition: April 2019

« Book Formatting by Derek Murphy @Creativindie »

CONTENTS

THE STRUGGLE IS REAL

You are not alone and there is hope if you struggle with parenting anger

Years ago, another mom stopped by with her boys, so our kids could have a playdate and we could spend a few hours enjoying some coffee and fellowship. I didn't know this woman very well, but as we spent the afternoon getting to know one another, she offhandedly said to me, "Sometimes I just get so angry with my kids." It seemed she was taken aback that she had let those words slip out of her mouth until I quickly returned by saying, "I know. I have the same struggle."

Unfortunately, my open self-disclosure was not how this new friend had expected me to respond. She had braced herself for not being understood, or even worse a condemning remark. It's not a wonder why parenting anger is not a commonly discussed topic amongst homeschoolers or even parents in general.

To act shocked about anyone's struggle with sin is unbiblical.

1 Corinthians 10:13a clearly states that "No test or temptation that comes your way is beyond the course of what others have had to face." And, to think just because a subject is not discussed, it is not an issue, wouldn't explain why my anger talk, "Be Angry...And Train Your Kids" is the most well-attended of all my talks when I'm speaking at a conference.

Unfortunately, living in a Pinterest-perfect and Facebook-friendly world, we have lost touch with how imperfect we really are, and how much we need to be real with one another AND be real about our imperfect and fallen nature. Masking sin gets us nowhere. Only when we can admit the error is within us and it needs to be fixed, can we open our lives up to the healing and repair only God can do to change our sinful ways.

I would love to tell you my struggle with parenting anger was not destructive to my relationship with my children when it was at its worse, but I can't. I vividly remember the days when my children feared me. I would turn in shame and cry out to God to save me from my inability to control my outbursts. In those dark days, I saw no hope for change and no possibility for badly damaged relationships to heal. I searched and prayed desperately for God to do something...and slowly He did.

A Story of Healing

My story of healing and being taught by God how to harness my anger is an amazing testimony of God's grace and His ability to make something beautiful out of a mess that seemed beyond repair. I can truly say with great conviction "...God works for the good of those who love Him, who have been called according to his purpose." Romans 8:28

The refreshing part of giving my testimony is the hope I can share with others who find themselves stuck in this same struggle.

For these reasons, I am writing this book about parenting anger. I will be sharing with you what I learned about myself, what I learned about God, what I learned about my children, and how all this knowledge was brought together by God's wisdom and grace to restore our family and lead us towards God's bright future.

The contents of this book was originally published as a series of blogs on the SPED Homeschool website and part of the proceeds of the sale of this book goes to support the on-going mission of SPED Homeschool to equip parents to homeschool children with special educational needs.

Truly only God can take a situation that seems bleak and beyond repair and turn it into a tool He can use to heal broken relationships.

I can't wait to get started.

PARENTING ANGER DEMYSTIFIED

*Understanding is the first step
in the road to changing parenting anger habits*

Anger has a way of catching us off guard when we don't understand what causes it, and what decreases our ability to handle it appropriately. Therefore, I will be starting off by sharing typical causes and conditions for angry parent episodes. These scenarios can happen in basically any parenting situation, but I am especially sensitive to the extra-ordinary demands that special-needs homeschooling parents experience as that explosive making cocktail mix of scenarios is where my anger episodes hit their peak.

My hope is that this information will help you better understand yourself, where you can easily get tripped up, and what factors in your life can make it harder to deal with your anger appropriately.

Anger is Common and Not Sinful

Personally, I gauge sin based on God's word. So, during the height of my parenting anger struggle, I found the following verse from Ephesians encouraging, while at the same time completely confusing and discouraging.

> *"Be angry, and do not sin, do not let the sun go down on your wrath, nor give place to the devil."*
> Ephesians 4:26-27

I had the "be angry" part down pat but getting beyond my anger without sin seemed like an impossible task...especially if my anger had to be dealt with before the sun went down each day.

What time and study eventually revealed to me was the fact that I had little understanding of my human condition and what caused me to get angry. But, as I gained understanding, I found a greater ability to make peace with my tendency to get angry instead of always wishing it wasn't there.

Typical Causes of Anger

All This for Nothing

Parenting can sometimes feel like lots of work that gets you nowhere. Laundry and dishes pile up and fill machines just as fast as you empty them. And, if you're homeschooling a struggling learner, your efforts in that department can often feel stagnant too. Lack of progression can make your fuse very short, and this frustration can lead to anger.

Life is Not Fair

Unless you live in a bubble, avoid social media, and keep your acquaintances to only people whose lives and circumstances are nearly identical to yours, the comparison trap can be a cruel nemesis. This can be particularly true for a parent of a special needs child. When a child demands more time, attention, and energy, than a typical child their age, a parent can look around and find lots of things that just don't seem fair. This lack of perceived fairness can cause resentment, which can lead to anger.

I'm Under Attack

Have you ever felt the whole world is against you? It can seem the entirety of the world's problems have fallen on your doorstep and you don't have enough within you to even start shoveling your way out of the mess. The daunting pile of therapy visits, medical paperwork, eating protocols, insurance requests, sensory-overloading places your child can't handle, and all the other things a parent of a special needs child juggles on a typical day can make life seem like a war zone. A parent who lives amidst these attacks can start to live defensively, which can turn everything else in life into something that leads to anger.

If Only

We are not talking about dream vacations or winning the lottery, but being able to use the bathroom alone, or going out in public without your child having a meltdown and everyone looking at you like you are the worst parent on the planet. These deviations from our desired lifestyle can be downright defeating. As you constantly see the life you wish you were living slipping from your hands, it's hard to get back into the game and stay positive. Parents who feel constantly kicked down by life struggle to see anything positive about their child or life in general and this rejection can lead to anger.

<u>Ouch, That Hurts</u>

It's not enjoyable to be in pain. The fact is, that stepping on a Lego can be just as painful as breaking a bone. Pain is something we try avoiding at all costs, but it is unavoidable in life. Whether you or your child deal with a chronic illness that causes pain, or your child acts out physically and you get caught in the crossfire, physical pain can be elevated in a family with a special needs child, which can lead to anger.

Circumstances Elevate Anger

<u>Health</u>

Not getting enough rest, exercise, sunlight, or eating a poor diet is enough to easily make life more difficult to handle. Add in larger health issues, sensory sensitivities, and food intolerances and the body's ability to regulate anger can be greatly diminished.

<u>Living Conditions</u>

Some people don't mind excessive clutter, noise, or bright lights, but if your living conditions create the constant sensation of "nails on the chalkboard," then your ability to mentally focus to diminish greatly your ability to regulate anger.

<u>Finances</u>

Financial worries can easily undermine anyone's ability to handle life in a rational manner. Worry can consume your thoughts, drain your energy, and keep you from sleeping at night which clouds your judgment and your ability to regulate your anger.

Spiritual Unrest

Anxiety, fear, mistrust, judgement, unhappiness, hate, and unforgiveness leave us in a state of unrest because we take things upon ourselves that were only meant for God to handle. When we load ourselves up with these burdens, we are unable to carry smaller burdens and they get blown out of proportion. When this happens, anger flares.

Relationship Issues

Relationships can bring great joy, but they can also bring tremendous sorrow. If we have a compromised relationship, we can start to second guess our other relationships, blame ourselves for past relational blunders, and attempt to close ourselves off from life. But when we withdraw from people we also lose our support network and sounding boards. We can be angered about things our friends would have told us not to stress about.

I hope these scenarios I have shared with you have opened your eyes to what may cause anger to rear up in your life. In my next article I will be sharing about the parenting anger escape door God showed me and how it opened my eyes to how God can use anger as a tool for our good, and the good of our children.

THE PARENTING ANGER ESCAPE DOOR

Esaping a sinful response to parenting anger is as easy as taking the back door

I **am excited to have finally reached this chapter** because the information it contains was transforming in my parenting anger struggle and what finally opened my eyes to the escape door I never knew before than that God reveals in 1 Corinthians 10:13.

"No temptation has overtaken you except such as is common to man; but God is faithful, who will not allow you to be tempted beyond what you are able, but with the temptation will also make the way of escape, that you may be able to bear it."

I was familiar with the story of Jesus cleansing the temple in John 2, but one morning I realized this story held the key to escaping my ongoing battle with parenting anger. Since that day, these passages have become some of my favorite in the Bible, because they provided me the escape plan I had desperately prayed for every time I lashed out at my children.

If you are not familiar with this passage, here it is:

"Now the Passover of the Jews was at hand, and Jesus went up to Jerusalem. And He found in the temple those who sold oxen and sheep and doves, and the money changers doing business. When He had made a whip of cords, He drove them all out of the temple, with the sheep and the oxen, and poured out the changers' money and overturned the tables. And He said to those who sold doves, "Take these things away! Do not make My Father's house a house of merchandise!" John 2: 13-16

Problems Trigger Anger

First, I want you to notice something. Jesus saw a problem. If you are unfamiliar with the Jewish law and customs of the temple, it may seem like Jesus' reaction to the marketplace-type atmosphere was a bit extreme. But, when you learn that the money changers and animal sellers were taking advantage of the people with weighted scales and "temple-approved" animals for sacrifices towards their own advantage, the picture becomes a bit clearer.

Those who had come to fulfill God's command to worship Him

were being swindled by crooked merchants. These merchants were mocking God's laws and profiting off the people who had journeyed to Jerusalem to dedicate their Passover sacrifice. And it was this injustice that fueled Jesus' righteous anger.

Now, as parents, we don't have temples and merchants that make us angry, but we do have a lot of other things that trigger our anger and aggravate how we respond to anger-provoking situations. It may help to look back at those triggers and aggravators from the previous chapter.

Don't Take the Bait

The secret to not giving into these triggers is to train yourself to see them, identify them, and then disconnect from them.

When I am speaking to an audience, I use a rope to signify a trigger. When you see the rope and focus on the problem that is causing your anger to rise, you are tempted to go pick up the rope and neatly deal with the situation as you see fit, just like a fish snaps at bait on a fishing line.

At first, you may not realize acting upon your anger will tangle you in a sinful response. But, even if you have the initial willpower to step back from the situation for a moment, the more you focus on the problem before you, the greater the pull becomes to act upon it and handle it as you see fit.

This is the sinful trap that anger elicits. A temptation to act with a sinful response. To quickly deal with the problem on our own terms, bring justice to the problem we are faced with, and move on from the issue as quickly as we can is the natural human response. But, this is not God's way of handling problems or how He would desire for us to use the energy we have been given when we see a problem.

An Alternate Option

The key then to turning away from the temptation is NOT to pick up the rope, but instead, turn the other direction and do what Jesus did...braid a whip! Yes, you heard me right, but let me explain.

The next thing we need to notice from the John 2 passage is the word "when" and the actions that caused a time-lapse in the story. Verse 15 specifically says, "When He had made a whip of cords..." How long do you think it took to gather up long leather strips and braid them, considering the whip was enough of a threat to drive oxen and merchants out of the temple? It had to have been quite a while.

What do you think Jesus was doing while He was braiding? When I contemplated this situation, I was taken back to His habit of always talking to the Father, consulting in His plan and seeking what He was doing in the situation. So it would be most reasonable to consider that He was praying and seeking God's guidance on how to best handle the problem before Him.

Revealing the Escape Door

Anger comes with a load of energy, but that energy was never intended to be used to enact justice.

> *"Beloved, do not avenge yourselves, but rather give place to wrath; for it is written, 'Vengeance is Mine, I will*

repay,' says the Lord." Romans 12:19

So, what do we do with it? We use it for praying, pressing into God for His plan, and when we need to ensure that we don't reach out with our own method to take care of the issue, we busy our hands.

Now, you probably aren't going to braid a whip, but I am sure there are lots of things you can do while you are praying, watching, and listening for God's direction. Laundry, dishes, yard work, sweeping, vacuuming, cleaning the bathroom, you get where I am going. These things are great outlets for our anger energy.

And, in redirecting your energy, you have moved towards the escape door, grabbed its handle and have moved away from anger's sinful trap.

A Door to Godly Character

Your next thought may be the same as mine, "What about the child who was misbehaving that invoked my anger? What do I do with him while I am praying?" You will need to wait for my next article to learn how to handle your child's side of this scenario, but I promise you it will be well worth the wait.

For now, though, I want you to focus on finding those ropes that lead you to sinful parenting anger episodes. Identify them, label them, and practice turning away from them and busying your hands while you pray and seek God. Don't worry, your child will not turn to the dark side before we get back to addressing his/her issues, but you need to focus on yourself first before you are ready for the next step.

There is much fruit to be gained in taking your time and really working on these steps one at a time. The reason I say this is be-

Peggy Ployhar

cause the escape door is not a door to nowhere, but a gateway to developing godly character in both you in your children.

So, be encouraged and keep pressing forward.

SHIFTING MODES: CONTROLLING TO TRAINING

*Shifting your habits to choose a
better path can change everything*

Once *I discovered how God's escape* door for my ugly anger episodes could help both me and my children, I have never looked at my sinful nature the same. I hope what I share with you as we continue delving into this topic will leave you feeling the same about your struggle and encourage you to keep pressing on.

"But as for you, you meant evil against me; but God meant it for good, in order to bring it about as it is this day, to save many people alive." Genesis 50:20

Yes, God makes wonderful masterpieces out of life's messes, and I am excited to share with you how He does just that with our misdirected parenting anger.

Blurred Vision

Once I started training myself to not pick up the rope and instead turn to braiding the whip (remember chapter 3?), my parenting vision cleared up considerably.

Anger had blurred my perception of effective parenting strategies. Instead of working productively to train my children, my desire to control their actions slowly crushed their spirits. When I finally stepped back, it was glaringly clear how much I needed to change my approach.

A Natural Warning Light

But checking our own behavior is only half the battle. The other half comes when we confront training our children due to the lack of character we are alerted to in their lives.

A lack of godly character will always make our internal righteousness meter go haywire. This is God's way of showing us we need to take notice of a situation which lacks godly character.

And, if you remember from the last article in this series, indicates a lesson needs to be taught.

Taking God's parenting anger escape door leads us to the perfect starting place where this character training lesson should start. We first pray and use our energy to seek God and His training lesson, and in doing so we discover the most impactful and eventually fruitful way to help our children develop strong godly character.

Building Solid Boundaries

When I am speaking to a group and get to this part in my talk, I take out three objects: a shoebox, a flat piece of cardboard, and a ping-pong ball. First, I show my audience how the ping-pong ball is extremely difficult to keep on top of the flat piece of cardboard. I point out how the lack of edges on the board leaves nothing to stop the ball from going off the edge. Then, I contrast that example with a ping-pong ball being securely held inside the shoebox, making sure to point out the high sturdy sides that allow this containment.

I use these examples because I want parents to understand that as we teach our children lessons in godly character, we are essentially giving them a building block to add to their natural boundaries. For a child instructed in righteousness, and given lots of building blocks, they instinctively know when to stop (just like the ping-pong ball) because those walls have been built over time and through many independent lessons that have stacked up sturdy boundaries for godly living. But, for a child who is only held back from the edge and controlled from doing wrong, they are not provided those blocks and instead when left without someone to hold them back from the edge will topple off just like the ping-pong ball on the flat piece of cardboard.

My demonstration may seem too extreme for those of you who have a younger child who is still close by and working on these skills, but when your child grows into his/her teen years and then moves into adulthood, you will realize how critical it is to have laid boundaries with strong and solid blocks of godly character. Those boundaries will spare you and your child much larger heartaches and pain than the training process could ever bring into your lives.

In the next chapter, I will be giving you some very practical how-to instructions on instilling godly character using these blocks. But, as you move on in this book, make sure you keep working on walking away from the rope, braiding the whip and seeking God for a clearer vision of how He is alerting you to character flaws through your natural anger meter. With a resolute desire to seek His escape door and readiness to grow in godly character along with your children, you will be well on your way to conquering your parenting anger.

INSTILLING GODLY CHARACTER

Shifting your habits to choose a better path can change everything

Parenting anger can point out a child's lack of character as I alluded to in the previous chapter. The other point I touched on is that if we seek to take God's route in using anger provoking instances, we can use it to effectively instruct our children towards godly character.

Yes, anger CAN instill godly character in your children...here is how.

Godly Character

If you were to look up a list of godly character traits, you may find a list like this:

Attentiveness

Obedience

Orderliness

Honor

Trust

Stewardship

Patience

Inquisitiveness

Responsibility

Generosity

Courage

Wisdom

Loyalty

Cooperation

Determination

Honesty

Self-control

Resourcefulness

Joy

Effectively Teaching Godly Character

The standard approach to teaching children about godly character is to give them a lesson or teach them what the Bible says about why it is important to live in this manner. But, as you and I both know, devoting weeks to a unit study on a specific character trait is way less effective than even a few perfectly timed lessons that speak directly to a child's heart.

This is where your anger comes in and points specifically at places where these lessons for each of your children will be most effective. So instead of looking at every anger-provoking instance you have with your children as a distraction or inconvenience, they instead should be perceived as doorways into teachable moments to perfect their character. This is that escape door.

Looking Practically at Character

Stop and think for a moment. What is something one of your children does that triggers your biggest anger response? Now, relate that anger trigger to a lack of character in your child.

Here's an example:

You may have a child who angers you when you find his toys lying around the house.

I would say, not only does this child lack "orderliness," but also "stewardship," "honor" (as others are required to step over the toys), and "responsibility."

Thus, this child needs to be taught his issue is much deeper than his inability to pick up toys. Instead, the greater lesson he needs to understand is his lack of character.

A Simple 3-Step Process

How do you start teaching this lesson? It is simple if you start implementing these three steps:

Step 1: Speak It

Start using the words "orderliness," "stewardship," "honor," and "responsibility" or whatever lack of a godly character trait mostly contributes to your child's poor behavior. Using these words on a regular basis not only implants them into your child's vocabulary but also normalizes their use in general conversation.

Step 2: Point It Out

Be on the lookout for ways these godly character traits are displayed by both your child AND other people. Point out positive or negative displays of godly character. As you label these displays, help your child to dissect these observations so he/she will also learn how to spot character first and actions second.

You can also create scenarios for your child to observe by acting them out. Employ the use of other family members, puppets, or stuffed animals and act out what a specific godly character trait looks like when it is being shown positively or negatively.

Step 3: Discuss It

Then, removed from the observed situation (further removed if it was an instance involving your child's lack of godly character), it is time to discuss the situation.

Now, I understand that based on your child's cognitive ability this task may require prompting, leading questions, or a parent asking questions and answering them while the child listens. All those methods are effective. The goal is not to have your child provide a detailed understanding of the situation, but rather to guide his/her thinking towards the truth embedded in the situation.

Hinging Lessons to a Solid Foundation

When I was working with my children in teaching them godly character in this manner I soon realized this process wasn't going to happen overnight. In fact, some days our homeschooling lessons were completely set aside so we could focus on character training.

I kept my sanity during those years by focusing on the purpose of those building blocks I spoke about in the previous chapter and that training my children was not dependent upon my ability to teach these lessons perfectly or even effectively. Instead, God had tasked me with being obedient in teaching the lessons when they presented themselves and hinged them to His immovable foundation...the Word of truth.

Each time we got to step 3 and started our discussion, my Bible (or an applicable verse I had memorized) was nearby. It got to a point where my oldest once said to me, "Mom, why do you always bring the Bible into everything?" My response, "Because life is about God, not us."

The sooner a child can be moved from a self-centered existence, the easier it is for him/her to rest within the safe boundaries godly character provides. A child who is self-focused will always see godly character as restricting or limiting. If you have a child who constantly fights against your instruction, then getting below the foundation of God's truth into the dirt of your child's heart is where your character training focus must focus first.

Digging Deeper

Instilling truth into a child's heart depends completely on how prepared his/her heart is to receive truth. In my next chapter, I am going to start walking you through the process on how to effectively "till" the soil of your child's heart.

Hang in there. I promise every moment God opens a door for you to teach godly character to your child and use the anger He has given you to fuel that teaching, He will take your efforts and multiply them in your child's life, even if your instruction is going to involving some digging before the foundation can be laid and the walls can be built.

CULTIVATING A CHILD'S HEART FOR INSTRUCTION

A bountiful crop requires more than good seed and the right conditions

It's extremely important to understand that instilling truth into a child's heart depends completely on how prepared his/her heart is to receive truth. Therefore, these next six chapters will focus on practical ways to cultivate a child's heart for truth. I will be basing everything I discuss in these chapters upon the previous methods shared in the first part of this book.

PARENTAL INTEGRITY

Building trust requires a focused effort
especially when it's been compromised

My prayer is as we slowly work through each of these steps, you will find how practical and healing God's way of handling our parenting anger can be when we use it towards building godly character in our children. Also, as you apply each of these cultivating steps, you will see how they work to bridge relational gaps that parenting anger may have created in your home. So, we start with ourselves: parental integrity.

Integrity and Trust

The reason I start with integrity is that a child only accepts a parent's instruction as much as they can trust that parent. Also, integrity is essential in breaking the protective crust a child builds up when situations have trained them to distrust...which often happens when a child lives with a parent who has a short fuse.

If a child can trust their parent, they will gladly absorb what that parent has to teach. Everything we teach our children hinges upon how much they trust us. If we fail to work on this basic foundation of our relationship with our child, much of our home-schooling and parenting instruction will be for naught. We are also more likely to see our children look to other places for truth instead of looking to us. Over time the relationships we were hoping to so tightly control with our misdirected anger will be the first things we lose the ability to influence.

An Integrity Check

A person of integrity is someone who can be trusted to do what they say they are going to do. They are not someone who uses excuses and their actions and lives are aligned with the priorities they say they value. Day in and day out, no matter what, a person with integrity can be trusted. This doesn't mean they are perfect, but it does mean they are really trying all the time.

Let me ask you, is this how your children see you? Do you live in a manner consistent with your public persona? Or, do you change your character once you get behind closed doors or within the safe sanctuary of your home and family?

Children will determine how trustworthy their parents are based on what they see them do and how they live either according to their word or apart from it. What a parent says about who they are, holds very little weight if it differs from how their child sees them behave.

Reversing Your Parental Integrity

I admit that as a young parent I did a very poor job of establishing integrity with my children. My anger was the biggest obstacle to developing integrity with my children because while I would tell them I loved them, I would not act in accordance with my words when I blew my top.

As I started sorting out my anger issues, I decided to make a concerted effort to build up my integrity in the eyes of my children. To do this, I first created a mantra, "I love you no matter what." And then I lived it out, by God's grace, one day at a time...praying a lot along the way. I followed the process of taking steps to work through my anger episodes just as I talked about at the beginning of this book.

My oldest son tested this new approach more than his siblings because he and I shared many ugly battles where I was not able to keep my integrity in check. Yet, every time he did something to push me, I followed the pattern of identifying my trigger, keeping myself busy and praying, looking for God's escape door, shifting my focus, and seeking the lessons that needed teaching while at the same time telling him, "I love you no matter what."

I wish I could say my son started believing me right away, but it took months of repeating this cycle and him testing the boundaries of my ability to act towards him just as I said I would. But, then the day came and the memory of this transformation in his heart still brings tears to my eyes.

It was a beautiful summer day and we were outside playing in the yard when my son again tested my integrity boundaries. I can't even remember what he did, but what I do remember was what he did and said after I told him, "I love you no matter what," and followed through with my anger in check.

He put his chubby hands on his hips and looked straight into my eyes and said to me, "You really mean it don't you?" From that day on things started to change in how I was able to speak into my son's life. No, he didn't stop testing my boundaries, but he did start trusting me.

I encourage you if you feel like all hope is lost with your children because of your past inability to handle your anger, there is a way to repair those relational gaps and instilling integrity is the first step in the healing process.

HUMBLE AUTHORITY

*Humble service can heal the greatest
fractures between a parent and child*

*C*hildren will often close their hearts towards parents who have habitually lashed out at them in anger, but it helps to also understand that even children who have been severely abused by a parent desire to see this bond restored. Don't lose heart. This process requires a lot of change in you and your relationship with your child, but every step of progress is a step towards the healing of fractures you have in your parent-child bond.

A Flipped Perspective

Authority's orientation from a human perspective is upside down when compared with God's viewpoint on this issue. After washing his disciples' feet, Jesus said the following about authority:

> "You call Me Teacher and Lord; and you are right, for so I
> am. If I then, the Lord and the Teacher, washed your feet,

you also ought to wash one another' feet. For I gave you an
example that you should do as I did to you."

(John 13: 13 – 15)

From God's point of view, authority comes from the bottom up, not the top down. It is asserted through humble service, not a dictating decree.

An Example of Authority

Consider this example: Say you were starting a new job where you had the ability to pick one of the two managers you could work for, and who would ultimately be given authority over your working environment. Here is how Manager A and Manager B say they operate their departments:

Manager A likes everything to be done her way. She has all the processes in place, and that is good because she has spent a lot of time making sure those processes are the most efficient way to do the job. As an employee working for her, Manager A just asks that you follow the procedures, get your work done, and work the system she has developed to the utmost of your capability. She knows her tried and true ways are the best at getting things done and is glad to have you fill one of the roles on her well-oiled team.

Manager B loves to see people work together, so much so he is willing to roll up his sleeves and help when needed. Manager B also has put together some well thought out procedures, but he also knows he can't think of every scenario where people and processes can be most efficient. Because of this, he desires to get the input from his team members on ways the processes can be improved and built into better and more efficient procedures for getting the job done. He knows each employee can contribute to the working environment, and he welcomes your input as a member of his close-knit team.

Which Would You Choose?

Looking at those two examples, which manager would you give the most authority to by taking the job under his/her command? If you are like most people, you would say Manager B because he leads through humble service, not as a dictator like Manager A.

Unfortunately, angry parents are often stuck in a similar dictating mode like Manager A when it comes to dealing with their children. And, even though they don't desire to handle interactions with their kids in this manner, sometimes old habits are hard to break. Instead of trying to break an old habit, I found creating a new habit to fill its place was much more effective. Thus, began my servanthood authority turnaround strategy.

A Turnaround Strategy

I created a servant strategy with each of my children by focusing on an activity each boy cared deeply about. For my oldest, that activity was Lego building which I personally found quite enjoyable. But with my second child, playing superheroes and dressing up in costumes was a bit more of a stretch. But, these activities were not about my enjoyment, they had a greater purpose – to connect with my children and show them I was willing to get down on their level to understand them better.

Over time my children started to realize I wanted to interact with them more like Manager B from the example above. When we were spending time playing together, we were also deepening our relationship. These relational bridges developed as we played together strengthened my boys' abilities in releasing authority of their lives to me. This transition did not happen because I demanded it, but rather because over time each one started to understand I really grasped who they were. Our time interacting helped me to get to the root of what they liked and how they thought, and thus they realized I really did have their best interest in mind when making the decisions I needed to make in parenting and teaching them.

It is never too late to start a turnaround strategy with your child. Be purposeful in building relational bridges by getting involved in what your child is interested in, no matter how much of a stretch that is for you. You will never regret invested time and energy to reconnect with your child.

UNCONDITIONAL ACCEPTANCE

There's powerful holding force in
being accepted even when we mess up

*T**his next step is the glue which helps* hold the integrity and authority changes I talked about in the previous two chapters in place. But first, here is why unconditional acceptance plays such an essential role in repairing any disconnect with your child when your parenting anger has caused division in the past.

Judgment by Reaction

Looking at our children through a nonjudgmental lens can be very difficult. We tend to have strong feelings for how much we desire to see our children succeed. These strong feelings can easily be read by a child through nonverbal communication. When our body language shows we are nervous, stressed, or even bothered when a child fails, our reaction passes along judgmental overtones. These reactions, if repeatedly observed by a child, will convey a parent's inability to accept failure even without any verbal communication.

Most of the time when we struggle with accepting our child's weaknesses, it stems from our own inability to accept our failures. If you struggle in this area, and in accepting yourself for being less than perfect, then the first thing you need to realize is that failure is an essential part of life which helps us, and our children grow and learn.

Embracing Failure

A while back I wrote an article for the SPED Homeschool website called Failing to Learn. In this article, I stressed the importance of learning how to accept failure as part of the learning process so mistakes can be launching points for more learning instead of roadblocks of further exploration and understanding.

With each mistake, we are given the opportunity to see how and why we failed. From there, we must choose to take what we learned in failing, and joyfully move forward in the hope that our next attempt will be better than our last based on what we learned in the last go-around.

When we can change our perspective about failure, the mechanics of accepting our children also becomes much easier. We are more prone to say "oops" when mistakes happen. And, our child's limitations are given flight to become vehicles for greater discoveries.

When we start to make this shift towards accepting a child's limitations and working on our responses to their failures, we also need to change our approach in how we redirect our child's reaction to their failures. This is where the big change in your parenting needs to happen to glue all these elements together...and to prepare for the final steps in cultivating your child's heart.

The Boxing Ring

When a child sees your reactions to their failures as an attack, you, in turn, will become the object for any out-lash in dealing with internal feelings of inadequacy. You essentially become your child's punching bag because your reaction comes with a dual meaning. First, it conveys to your child you are safe because your love for them is what caused your reaction to their failure, but secondly, you are also an enemy because your reaction has placed you in their battle zone. Thus, instead of your child taking on the real issues he/she is facing, exposed through failure, your child makes the issue about your relationship.

If you were to view this scenario as a boxing ring, your child would be in the battle of life with you in the same ring. There are many things your child battles each day, but your job as a parent was never to be his opponent. Instead, you have been called to be a coach who can provide fighting strategies for all the important things he fights through in life.

Coaching to Success

By accepting your child's fight as part of the learning process, and your role as the ever-vigilant coach through this training period in your child's life, your goal will be to remove yourself from the ring by accepting your child and battles they are up against. Win or lose, you must show you are willing to stick it out while learning alongside what works and what doesn't with failure, and success, leading to the winning strategies.

Each time your child tries to get you into the ring, you must make a dedicated effort to keep your feet out of the battle zone. And when needed, calling a "time-out" a break until your child is ready to receive training instead of taking you on in the ring. Over time this process will become easier, especially as your child starts to see the value of having you working with them to fight these struggles instead of being frustrated, embarrassed, or upset when they fail.

FORGIVENESS & MERCY

*We need forgiveness to move
on and mercy to give us hope
for our future mistakes*

Forgiveness is much easier to conceptualize in theory than apply in real life. Emotions, past experiences, and desires to control our circumstances as well as others muddy the waters. When it comes to forgiving others, our natures cling to the hurts, harms, or unpleasant memories more than they desire to forgive someone.

The reality is, no one is perfect, and therefore we all have the potential to hurt one another. Forgiveness is a mode we must learn to live in and live in with peace. In blog series on childhood depression I wrote for the SPED Homeschool website, I described my Cyclical Perfection Wheel as a way God actually uses our need for forgiveness to perfect us through the process of sanctification. The goal of living our imperfect lives as parents is to show our children that we not only can forgive them, but we can also accept forgiveness ourselves.

Judgment Doesn't Lead to Forgiveness

When parents struggle with anger, it often stems from judging right/wrong, good/bad, devious intentions/poor choices and making many more "assumptions" instead of holding out for God's truth in a situation. This immediate need to resolve a situation based on human assumptions can lead children to believe mistakes of any kind are not permissible or forgivable. Over time, many children take on this judgmental burden and apply it to themselves without even knowing they are perceiving their world through this judgmental lens.

Judgment leaves no open door for forgiveness. Instead, self-condemnation fueled by misguided assumptions pull both parent and child away from receiving God's mercy and complete forgiveness. Our parental fears push our children further away from us and in doing so make us their opponents instead of their coaches, as in the boxing ring example mentioned in the previous chapter. So, while we think we are fighting to help our children battle life's obstacles, we instead become the greatest obstacle in their path because of how we are judging their behavior.

Judgment Skews Truth

When we get angry and allow our judgment to lead the way on how we respond to our children's behavior, we don't leave room for the whole truth of a situation to come to light before we react. Often, when we wait to allow the whole truth to surface, we find our judgment was extremely skewed, and any response at the moment would have made the situation worse instead of better.

Recently I received a desperate call from a mother whose son had been cheating on his school work and lying to both her and others about his progress. The mother's first response to me was to ask what possible outside influences her son must have recently gotten mixed up in to cause him to change his behavior so dramatically. Her perception was that based on her son's past behavior this sudden change must be someone else's fault.

In talking more with this mother, I found out her son was under a lot of pressure and his actions were more in line with a depressed and anxious teen than one who was acting rebelliously. I explained to her that even though she perceived her son's lying and cheating as a malicious act, from the perspective of a depressed teen his actions were more likely self-preserving. Without trying to be devious to those who cared for him, his anxiety over what his future holds after high school was causing him to act in a way that would keep his world in a place he felt he could survive. His lying and cheating, although not the best means to create a safe bubble, were allowing him to stay in a place he felt he could control and could distance himself from his fears.

Truth Opens the Door for Mercy and Forgiveness

Looking at a situation in truth allows our hearts to see beyond judgment. This is what mercy is all about. Mercy is the opposite of judgment, but mercy is the necessary first step in bringing us to a place where we can forgive and receive forgiveness. In the example above, both mother and son must see the truth of how depression, anxiety, and assumptions are skewing their ability to work together towards fighting the battle ahead. But, mercy is not a one-way street. Even if this mother does her best to see her son's battle from a merciful perspective, she can't change her son's ability to accept this mercy for himself.

Many times, we struggle with our inability to control our children and their decisions. Angry parent responses are often triggered by the desire to control our children. Thus, allowing our children to struggle and fail while we patiently coach them, pray for them, and forgive them is one of the toughest transitions parents must make to help children start the process of receiving forgiveness for their own failings.

Learning to forgive as well as accepting forgiveness takes time and lots of prayers. Mercy is often the step we try to skip in the forgiving process because it's the most difficult part of forgiving; it requires us to let go of controlling the outcome and, at the same time, to fight our desire to judge. But we win this fight by praying for eyes to see others the way God sees them.

Allowing Forgiveness to Be the New Norm

As a child's heart softens, he learns over time to be less judgmental of mistakes. Judgment is replaced by the life-giving response of giving and receiving mercy and forgiveness. This transition opens children's hearts for instruction because mercy is the new norm instead of fear of judgment. Children who operate under the umbrella of mercy learn to embrace their mistakes as ways to learn as well to grow closer to their all-forgiving Father.

As parents, we also need to live in a state of mercy and forgiveness. We need to realize how our past actions towards our children, as well as how judgmental we have been of our own lives, is not healthy. God's forgiveness heals any wounds our sinful actions have created. He even turns those wounds into some of the most powerful places from which we can minister to share His hope. But, asking your children to forgive you and accepting forgiveness is where the healing must start. Then, it must continue with restorations, which I will talk about in my next article in this series as we dive into the importance of honor.

I hope you embrace the forgiveness God has for both you and your children, and the merciful perspective He has to share with you on how He views each of your lives.

HONOR

Honor is something we must earn,
especially when it's been compromised

*I*n restoring relationships with my children after the healing process began with my parenting anger issues, the primary focus of my actions concentrated on being worthy of their honor. Asking their forgiveness was only the first step in this process. The rest of the wide divide my anger had created between myself and my children required more than lip-service, it required action. And, my actions needed to show my heart was changing and willing to take responsibility for the effects of my post-anger aftermath.

An Act of Kindness

How did I do that? Well, it started slowly, but began with a new something in our house called a "re-honor job." I took it upon myself to be the first to take on these "jobs." Through them, I demonstrated these jobs were a means for restoring broken relationships. And having done more than my fair share of destruction, due to my parenting anger episodes, I realized it was up to me to start the restoration process.

Every time I did something to dishonor a child, I followed up with asking forgiveness and doing a "re-honor job," a physical act of kindness. This physical act worked as a bridge to start spanning the gulf created by the many years of inappropriate actions taken towards my children. As I learned to let go of my anger and harness it properly, as well as use these "re-honor jobs" to start repairing relationships, I also started incorporating these "jobs" in my child training, to ensure even the smallest relational fractures were repaired within our home.

An Example

I will provide you with a scenario to illustrate how these "jobs" worked into our family life and child training. The following scenario played itself out many times in our early years of homeschooling. In general, this is how it went:

Boys will be boys. If you have boys, more than likely they fight as much as mine did. It really didn't matter what the fight was about, but one would say or do something to get the other riled, and a fight would ensue.

As I stated earlier, my general policy was not to get involved in my children's fights. But, when the outcome was not being worked out on their own accord (or there was the potential of blood being drawn), I stepped in. Usually, my intrusion was only long enough to bring them into the kitchen, assign them each a chair, and remind them not to leave their chairs until they'd forgiven one another.

Sometimes they followed (even begrudgingly was fine with me), but if not, they knew I would bring it up later, so often my wishes were followed without complaint. Once in the kitchen, and after making sure they were settled, I would give them my reminder and take my leave. Now, I didn't go very far...just another room where I was within ear-shot, but out of their line-of-sight.

Depending on the day, and their attitudes, my boys would either agree to forgive one another immediately, or they would start a very long and drawn out shouting battle across the kitchen. Either way, at the end of their dialogue, the two would agree to forgive one another and call me into the room to let me know they'd settled their argument.

Now, I must point out that, if a child got out of his chair during the process of working out his differences with his brother, he knew this was an issue he would have to take up with me afterward, which I will explain in just a moment.

At the point peace was declared and I was beckoned into the kitchen, if one or both had not followed me to the kitchen without a fight or if anyone had gotten up from their assigned chair before receiving permission to leave, I would ask that child(ren) if they were also willing to ask my forgiveness for their disobedience towards me. Additionally, if I had lost my cool during any point of the process, I made sure to also ask forgiveness.

After forgiveness was given at the kitchen level, we took it to a higher house and prayed together asking God to forgive and restore. And then we did "re-honor jobs."

An Opportunity

These jobs were to be physical manifestations of our desire to restore the relationships our actions had damaged. Often the boys would do a small chore or clean up something for their brother. On the other hand, if the re-honor job was directed at me, they would usually do something I normally did around the house. And, if I was re-honoring a child(ren) then I did a chore(s) to restore the honor I had compromised with my son(s).

What our family learned through these exercises over the years was it has never become easy to re-honor someone. Saying "Sorry" or "Please forgive me" can become meaningless words, but physically honoring another person requires us to bow our lives during each act of kindness to serve that person and elevate them above ourselves. And, with that bow, healing and restoration happen and the sin which compromised that relationship is snuffed out by love.

When we honor another person, we put ourselves into a submissive position which says, "I have chosen to place you ahead of my own desires and will."

An Established Pattern

Honor is a tricky thing in relationships – it needs to be earned, but it also needs to be maintained. I pray that if you are in the process of healing the relationships in your family because of your own struggles with parenting anger that you work to re-establish honor starting with yourself and then work the concept into your child training process.

Honor truly is a key element to cultivating your child's heart for instruction and it comes through living out forgiveness by purposefully building in acts of kindness, or "re-honoring jobs", into your training.

TIME MANAGEMENT

*Methodically releasing control of
scheduling your child's life*

Over the years of working through my parenting anger issues, the biggest lesson I have learned about myself is my natural tendency to want to always be in control. I have talked about letting go of control in many areas of parenting throughout this series; control of my children's character development, as well as my parenting approach in respect to my use of authority, of conveying acceptance, in providing forgiveness, and with my desire to restore honor. The final, and most deceptively hidden, area I needed to surrender my need to over control as a parent was time management.

Finding Balance in Time Management

Controlling every single moment of every single day in my children's lives was not healthy. Plus, if my goal was to help my children learn the skill of managing their time effectively they needed opportunities to practice. Opportunities I was denying them by always micro-managing their schedules.

My blindness to my overly controlling approach towards my children's schedules was aided by the fact that all my children deal with varying degrees of executive functioning deficits. These deficits limit their natural abilities to quickly and efficiently schedule, plan and organize themselves. So, as a mother who is naturally gifted in this area, it was easy to just step in and take over these responsibilities for my children instead of letting go and teaching them to take ownership for their own use of time.

For any parent of a struggling child, the tendency to overcompensate and take control is a constant battle. On one hand you desire for your child to learn and grow, but on the other hand the pain this struggle causes your child and often your own self (extra messes to clean up, extended length in completing tasks, etc.) is much more easily alleviated by stepping in. How then is a parent to win over this desire to control while still keeping a child on track? The answer is balance.

A balanced time-management approach involves evaluating three things: your child, your approach, your tools. Looking at these three areas and then determining a balanced plan on how to appropriately give your child the help needed to get through a regular schedule while developing time management skills of their own along the way.

Understanding Your Child

Understanding the true capability if your child to manage time is critical when figuring out how much this child can manage realistically without your help. Have you ever done a critical analysis of how well your child can break down a larger task into a checklist of smaller parts to complete the whole project?

One easy way to figure out your child's executive functioning capability is to test it by asking your child to do a task which requires multiple steps. I would suggest doing this test with different types of tasks because children often have a greater ability to focus and plan when they are interested in the task (like building a Lego set) than they do when they are disinterested in a task, like cleaning the bathroom.

If you have an older student, you can also use this free time management quiz (https://www.mindtools.com/pages/article/newHTE_88.htm). The quiz has 15 simple questions your student can answer, and then the website provides ideas for goal setting based on the deficiencies revealed by the quiz.

Developing Your Approach

Now that you know what skills your child has for managing his own time, and which ones you need to help teach for greater mastery, you should develop a strategy for teaching time management skills. Here are some website with great resources on helping kids with mild time management issues, moderate executive functioning issues, or even more severely limited scheduling abilities.

Mild Time Management Strategies

11 Easy Tips for Teaching Your Kids Time Management
(https://www.verywellfamily.com/how-to-teach-your-kids-time-management-skills-4126588)

The Age-By-Age Guide to Teaching Kids Time Management
(https://www.scholastic.com/parents/family-life/parent-child/teach-kids-to-manage-time.html)

6 Ways to Teach Time Management Skills
(https://flintobox.com/blog/child-development/teach-kids-time-management-skills)

Moderate Executive Functioning Strategies

Graphic Organizers from the Learning Disabilities Foundation of America (https://ldaamerica.org/graphic-organizers/)

Helping Kids Who Struggle with Executive Functioning (https://childmind.org/article/helping-kids-who-struggle-with-executive-functions/amp/)

10 Frightfully Useful Tips from Executive Functioning Coaches

(https://www.beyondbooksmart.com/executive-function-ing-strategies-blog/adhd-awareness-month-top-10-tips-from-executive-function-coaches)

5 Must-Have Apps for Improving Executive Functioning in Children (https://www.beyondbooksmart.com/executive-functioning-strategies-blog/5-great-apps-for-improving-executive-function-ing-in-children)

Strategies for Students with Severely Limited Scheduling Abilities

Tactile Schedules for Students with Visual Impairments and Multiple Disabilities (http://www.pathstoliteracy.org/strategies/tactile-schedule-students-visual-impairments-and-multiple-disabilities)

8 Types of Visual Student Schedules (http://theautismhelper.com/10-types-visual-student-schedules/)

Object Schedule Systems (http://www.perkinselearning.org/videos/teachable-moment/object-schedule-systems)

Free Printable Visual Schedules (https://www.behaviorinbalance.com/visual-schedules-autism-kit/)

Utilizing Your Tools

Based on how much help your child needs and what approach you feel would best help in teaching better time management, you can now start putting together your tools. The various articles links above are filled with everything from digital tools to very hands-on physical tools.

For our family, we did a lot of visual schedules on a huge blackboard in our kitchen when our children were very young. We supplemented that schedule with daily conversations about upcoming activities and plans to ensure our children remembered what lay ahead and weren't surprised when we had something planned that didn't fit into our normal routine. But, as our children grew older those schedules moved to student planners, apps, and shared documents along with the daily conversations.

Knowledge has great power. In my experience with letting go of controlling my children, knowing more about the type of help they needed and when I was becoming overly controlling greatly helped with restoring a proper parent-child relationship in our home.

CHANGING TO GOD'S WAY

*Change placed into God's hands
will always work out for good*

Too often we feel like once we've been given the information to change and move forward to resolve an issue we have been struggling with, we must figure out how to pull everything together and make it work. We set up the basic plans of the desired vision. Maybe offer up a quick prayer. And then, we plow on ahead. But, God has a better way. His desire is that you pray and then follow His perfect plan to work things out for good.

CHANGING THROUGH PRAYER

*Prayer ushers in the change we can't
bring into our lives without God's help*

As humans, we instinctively know we need to pray. When tragedy strikes we ask for prayer, we gather to grieve and cry out, and our hearts seek healing from beyond what we can see, feel, and touch. But, the biggest tragedy is that we don't practice praying much when things are going well in our lives. We forget we have needs and large voids we can't fill on our own. The biggest void I could not fill through my own self-determination was the one created by the damage my parenting anger had created in my own life and in my relationships with my children.

A Spiritual Battle

Parenting anger at its core is a spiritual battle, and therefore prayer is fundamental to changing parenting anger and bringing about healing, in both the parent and the child. Prayer alone brought forth this healing in my life. How? By ushering forgiveness and restoration to places grace alone could reach.

Prayer is about asking, but it is more than that. It is also about seeking something greater and desiring for it to come into our lives and change our nature; the nature which often brings us to the place where we realize our need for forgiveness and healing. And, prayer is about submitting to that change by pursuing it with tenacity rather than pursuing our natural inclinations or good intentions.

A Plea for Change

When I decided in my heart that I no longer wanted to live with the rages I often experienced, I started to pray for God to change my heart and to heal my relationships with my children with more vigor than I ever had before. My prayers went from "stop this" to "change me."

Change was slow, but every time God revealed a new lesson I then prayed for His help to heal me, change me, and restore me. When I backslid in carrying out this new lesson, I sought out His forgiveness as well as the forgiveness of my children, and we prayed together for God to help us accept His grace and do better the next time. I also started to make it a point to pray with my children when they met with failure in their own battles.

Fundamental to Change

Prayer was fundamental in keeping us moving forward, in giving us the strength to keep going on, to accepting our imperfect natures, and in realizing all the more our need for a Savior and a constant help as we navigated life with a desire to become less angry and hurt and more loving and compassionate—more like our heavenly Father.

My prayer for you is that you don't give up, on yourself or your children. The struggle to change and grow is worth the battle, and the best part is that God will be fighting right alongside you all the way. Savor the wisdom God shared with you through this healing process and allow the lessons to go not just to your head, but also your heart.

ALLOWING THE HOLY SPIRIT TO WORK

Greater things can be accomplished
when we allow the Holy Spirit to work

I *have always believed it has been my job* to live my life of faith before my children with excitement and to share with them the walk God has me on, especially as it affects their lives. As I pray and commit to Spirit-led parenting, the Holy Spirit does the heavy lifting of convincing, convicting, and moving my children's hearts.

A story I share often is when God had impressed upon both mine and my husband's hearts that He wanted us to sell our house and move to the county. For our oldest on the Autism spectrum, it seemed like a death sentence to leave behind his comfortable world for the unknown. But I trusted God had clearly spoken to me. One day when he was protesting about us preparing the house to sell, I decided to let the Holy Spirit do the heavy lifting of convincing my son this was God's will not mine.

I basically told my son, "You ask God to tell you if moving is something he wants our family to do, and then come back to me when you have clearly heard from him."

A few days later, unbenounced to me, he prayed to God to show him that day if we were supposed to move. All day long he was looking, but he never told anyone of his prayer for fear we would add in our own interpretations.

Then when evening rolled around, he went to his sister's room with his other brother to listen to an audio tape of "Mr. Henry's Wild and Wacky Bible Stories" as they did most evenings. It was their practice to not turn the light on because our daughter usually fell asleep during the story, so in the darkness, my son picked up a tape, put it into the tape player, and sat down with his siblings to listen.

Do you know what story he happened to put into the player that night? The story of Abraham being called out of his homeland. As soon as the words, "Abraham, get out of this land" hit my son's ears, he knew those words were the answer he had been looking for that day. He ran out of the room screaming at the top of his lungs, "Nooooo!" And that is when I was brought up to speed with the prayer and God's answer. Never again did he complain about moving.

We forget too often, no matter how old or young we are, we have access to the same God and the same Holy Spirit. Spirit-led parenting trusts God through the Holy Spirit to do the convincing, convicting, and moving of our children's hearts, and God's ways will always turn out more positively than when we try to force our will or our faith or God's ordained will upon our children.

GOD'S WORKING OF A GOOD ENDING

Our version of good will always miss the mark, but God's endings don't

When I get to the end of this talk, I bring up a slide with a current picture of my family. My husband Doug, of almost 25 years, my son Thomas (22), my son Tim (20), my daughter Maggie (14), and myself. I remind my audience about where the talk started and the detached relationships with my children I shared at the beginning of my presentation.

I am so very thankful to say this divide no longer exists. My boys, even as young adults, confide with me openly about their struggles, hopes, and dreams. They are even excited to spend time with me, desire for me to be one of the first people they share their good news with and seek me out when they are looking for someone to support and lift them up.

A Second Chance

My 14-year-old daughter entered our family after my parenting approach changed and therefore I was able to use the godly wisdom I've shared with you in this book when raising her. I cherish this gift God gave me which allowed me to see how differently parenting can look when using godly anger with wisdom for child training.

The funny thing is that when I share the stories I have shared with you in this book, my daughter doesn't have any recollection of these broken relationships in our family. She is witness to a truly transformed family and home has always been a safe and nurturing place.

Years ago I never would have believed that this dramatic of a transformation was possible for our family. But, that didn't mean I let my lack of faith get in the way of asking God to do the impossible. Instead, I clung to the scripture verse Phillippians 1:6 which says,

"...being confident in this very thing, that [God] who has begun a good work in you will bring it to completion in Christ Jesus."

I knew my children were EACH one of those "good works" and I reminded God, many times through my tears and laments, that from the beginning with stirring me to change my heart, He started something He alone could finish and I would keep asking, seeking, and knocking until He did.

A Good Work in Disguise

In looking back though I often found myself asking God, "Why did you allow my boys to start out their lives with an angry mother?" Then one day, God made it very clear to me how my anger was a necessary part of His "good work" in my boy's lives.

My middle son Tim, who at the time was about 7 years old, decided to try track and field as one of his summer activities. And, with afternoon meets my oldest son Thomas (9) and my daughter Maggie (2) came with me to root for their brother in his events.

On this same track team was my son Tim's best friend, the son of our church's pastor. I secretly envied his family. They homeschooled six children who were always obedient and who followed their parents like little ducklings wherever they went. Not exactly the scenario I lived out with my boys since we were in the midst of their heart cultivating process. Thus, my boys more often behaved then like a wild pack of dogs, instead of sweet ducklings.

At one of these afternoon meets, our pastor showed up alone with his two older boys, each of them the same ages as my boys, another younger son, and his newborn daughter. His wife occasionally came to the meets, but on this particular day, she and the other children were at an appointment.

As my pastor and I were talking and watching the meet, he realized he needed to go back to his car to change his daughter's diaper. He asked if I would be willing to watch his two other sons while he made a quick run to the parking lot. I gladly agreed and off he went with his daughter.

Then, all of a sudden the sky grew dark, and it started to pour. In fact, it started raining so hard it was difficult to see. The track meet came to a sudden halt. Kids were running everywhere, especially my pastor's children who were greatly distressed since they were unable to receive their usual guidance from a nearby parent.

My sons all of a sudden rose above the circumstance. They stepped into the chaos and took command. Without any help or urging on my part, they were yelling at kids to move towards them, to stop panicing and to get to the nearby shelter.

An internal strength my boys had developed as a result of being raised by a mom who struggled with anger was now being used by God to help others. As I stood and watched this whole event play out, I felt God whispering in my ear and saying, "This is why your boys had to go through those experiences. I needed them to be strong for what I had planned for their lives. Trust me. I am making their futures even better than any 'good' you can imagine."

Cling to Hope

As you look at your relationships with your children, the changes and the training yet ahead, never lose hope of the good work God is working out in your family too.

But also remember, we are all sinners and no matter how hard we try we will never be a perfect parent. Only God can fulfill that role.

In our parenting future, we are all bound to slip up and say or do something we wish we wouldn't have. In those times remember to ask for forgiveness, from both God and your child. Re-honor, and then resolve to learn and move on. This is what training is all about, for us our kids.

Yes, God has also begun a good work in your family's life. Trust His leading. Depend on Him to bring those "good things" to completion. And, never stop believing He has the ability to not only heal what's broken but use it as a testimony for His glory.

ACKNOWLEDGMENTS

This book is dedicated to my family. I thank God for each of you in my life and praise Him for the work He has done in the midst of our struggles together.

To my husband Doug, you are patient and loving beyond my comprehension. You have been a calm voice of wisdom when panic has overtaken me and a firm wake up when I needed to be set straight. But, I've always rested in the fact that your motivation for coming alongside me as my helpmate has been your devotion to our relationship and your unswerving love for me.

To my son Thomas, you are the sweetest young man and I love the time we are able to spend together. I am so proud of how you have learned to press on through the hard things in life and the resilience you have developed through those circumstances. God sees your heart and so do I. Keep pressing on and trust in the good that God has ahead for you.

To my son Tim, you amaze me every day. Your witty comments make me smile and your unique perspective on life is always refreshing to hear. I also love the fact that you are enjoying the process of discovering your distinct skills and talents. I know God has great plans for you and I pray that you will embrace those plans and allow God to use you for His glory.

To my daughter Maggie, you are a precious jewel in my life. Your heart to live for the Lord and your ability to see beauty in the most simple things are treasures I hope and pray you always hold dear. I love that we have been able to spend so much time with one another, travel together, work out on ariel silks with one another, and develop a home school curriculum around your interests and gifts.

I would also like to thank the SPED Homeschool team and board of directors.

I especially want to thank Mary Winfield and Tracy Glockle for all the time you volunteered to SPED Homeschool as editors for the blogs that were used in this book.

I would also like to thank my longtime friend and mentor, Dianne Craft. Thank you Dianne for always believing in me, encouraging me to use my gifts and follow God's call in my life.

Thank you also to Jan Bedell who has also become a wonderful mentor and friend since joining the SPED Homeschool board. Jan you have been a steadfast encourager in my life and I can't thank you enough for your consistent support and encouragement.

I would finally like to thank the many MOPS groups, homeschooling groups, and homeschool conference attendees over the years who sat through my talk "Be Angry..And Train Your Kids" and asked questions which spurred conversations and refined my talk, and eventually this book's final contents.

ABOUT THE AUTHOR

Peggy Ployhar, SPED Homeschool Founder & CEO, is a leader in the special education homeschooling community and a frequent writer and speaker on special education homeschooling issues. Peggy's journey into homeschooling started 17 years ago when her oldest child was diagnosed with Asperger Syndrome.

Peggy is the former THSC (Texas Home School Coalition) Special Needs Team Lead, MACHE (Minnesota Association of Christian Home Educators) Special Needs Coordinator and MOPS (Mothers of Preschoolers) Area Coordinator for MN, ND, and SD. She is certified by the American Association of Christian Counselors and trained as a Precept Bible Study leader.

You can tune in every Tuesday evening on the SPED Homeschool Facebook page to join Peggy as she hosts SPED Homeschool Conversations, a weekly talk show about special education homeschooling or you can join her daily on her personal YouTube channel, Daily Revelations.

In her spare time you will find Peggy immersed in a book, enjoying a paddle board ride, walking with her husband, or in her garage with her daughter doing the latest move she's learned on the ariel silks.

Peggy and her husband Doug live in League City, TX, where they still home school the youngest of their three children (22, 20, and 14).

If you would like to follow Peggy on social media, you can follow her public profile on Facebook, follow her on Twitter at @PeggyPloyar, or follow her YouTube channel Daily Revelations.

Peggy's articles can also be found on the SPED Homeschool website (spedhomeschool.com) which is where you can also find links to all the SPED Homeschool social media accounts, include the SPED Homeschool Facebook page where Peggy hosts the weekly broadcast, SPED Homeschool Conversations. Make sure to check out the events section of the Facebook page to view all the upcoming interviews.

You can also watch and listen to recorded broadcasts on both the SPED Homeschool YouTube channel or the SPED Homeschool podcast, which can be played/downloaded for free from iTunes, GooglePlay, Spotify, and Podomatic.

Thanks for reading! Please add a short review on Amazon and let me know what you thought!

Also, if you enjoyed this book and are looking to get a regular dose of similar content, make sure to subscribe to the monthly SPED Homeschool newsletter. Our newsletter not only highlights one of Peggy's devotional vlogs, but a listing of the newest content as well as current deals being offered by our partner organizations. You can find out subscribe button on the bottom of every page of the SPED Homeschool website, spedhomeschool.com.

We also appreciate your prayerful consideration in becoming a donor partner with SPED Homeschool to help us further our work of empowering special education homeschooling parents to help their students succeed. You can find out more by going to our giving portal at this link:

https://sped-homeschool.snwbll.com/giving-portal

Made in the
USA
Middletown, DE